Take wing over France and be
Touched by the beauty of the lands
Admiring markets laden with cheeses to buy
Taste and you too will understand

TASTING TO
ETERNITY

A love affair with traditional French cheeses.

David Nutt

For Annick on our thirty second year of marriage.

If I had a son that was about to marry, I would say to him: Beware of a young woman that does not like wine, truffles, cheese and music.

Colette

CONTENTS

THE POET...

THE GOURMAND...

THE EPICURE....

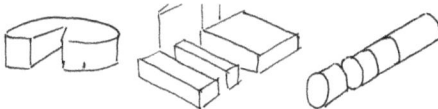

THE POET...

Cheese is the soul of the soil.
It is the purest and most romantic
link between humans and the earth.

Pierre Androuet

AN ODE TO CHEESE

Every time I see you gloating on plates

Showing off autumn's colors and particular shapes

My head spins; my taste buds awake

My eyes brighten with contemplation

My pulse quickens with expectation

My nose tickles with anticipation

Dare I touch your velvety coat?

Maybe just a gentle poke

Dare I slice you to the heart

To glory at your essential part?

Dare I take just one taste?

Oh! My love, will I be swept into pastoral lands?

Meadows dressed with mountain herbs

Grasses growing rich from spring rains

Weather patterns playing on the fields

Cattle grazing in nonchalant pose

Milk spilling from earthenware urns

This is your history and much more

Your form and shape are well defined

Your texture and colour always refined

Sometimes you are streaked with blue

Roquefort, Fourme d'Ambert or Bleu de Gex

Sometimes your odour is sensationally strong

Are you Maroilles, Salers or Munster?

Then, my love, your seductive power

Is but dulcet sonnets to my nose

Sending rhythms down to my toes

Now to taste

I take my time, lingering

Subtle, savoury, with a distinctive tang

Is this Camembert, Charolais, or Chabichou?

Goat, cow, or ewe?

Are you from the snow-capped mountains

Or the sun blessed plains?

You guard your secret well

But, by your taste I know

Artful as you are

Cunning, tantalizing and sensuous

My love, I detect distinctive signs

In the upper reaches of my palate

In the lower register of my tongue

I sense your secrets; I find my pleasure

You are without comparable measure

If only I could find some wine

All would be sublime.

Bibliothèque Nationale, Paris

COW'S CHEESES

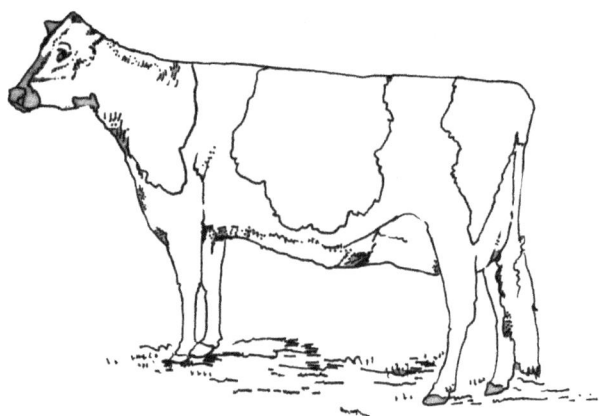

Funny beasts with docile heads
Hips all bones
Spindly legs, stomachs well fed
Hides of many hues
Piebald is considered pert
Tranquil they stand and chew the cud
Perched in mountain pastures
Or scattered on sun drenched domains
Grazing on grasses of fertile plains
Saucy milk in udders full
Milkmaids hurry with their stools
White and creamy their pails soon brimming
Experienced hands toil on the daily take
At night the milks lie still
Morning dawns with a different grain
Cheese, dear cows, you have done it again.

BEAUFORT

Floral Alpine pastures in mountain passes

Weather patterns that chase the clouds

Herds of cows in meadows painted with flowers

Their milks sweetened by the lush grasses

This cheese the Roman conquerors adored.

Huge in form, rind all beige

Dough of texture silky and firm

Summer milks an epicurean ecstacy

Scent and sapor of exceptional flavour

The palate caressed with temptation

Conveying dreams of Alpine chalets and milk galore

Taste slowly to fully sense its delicious core

No wonder the Romans were in awe.

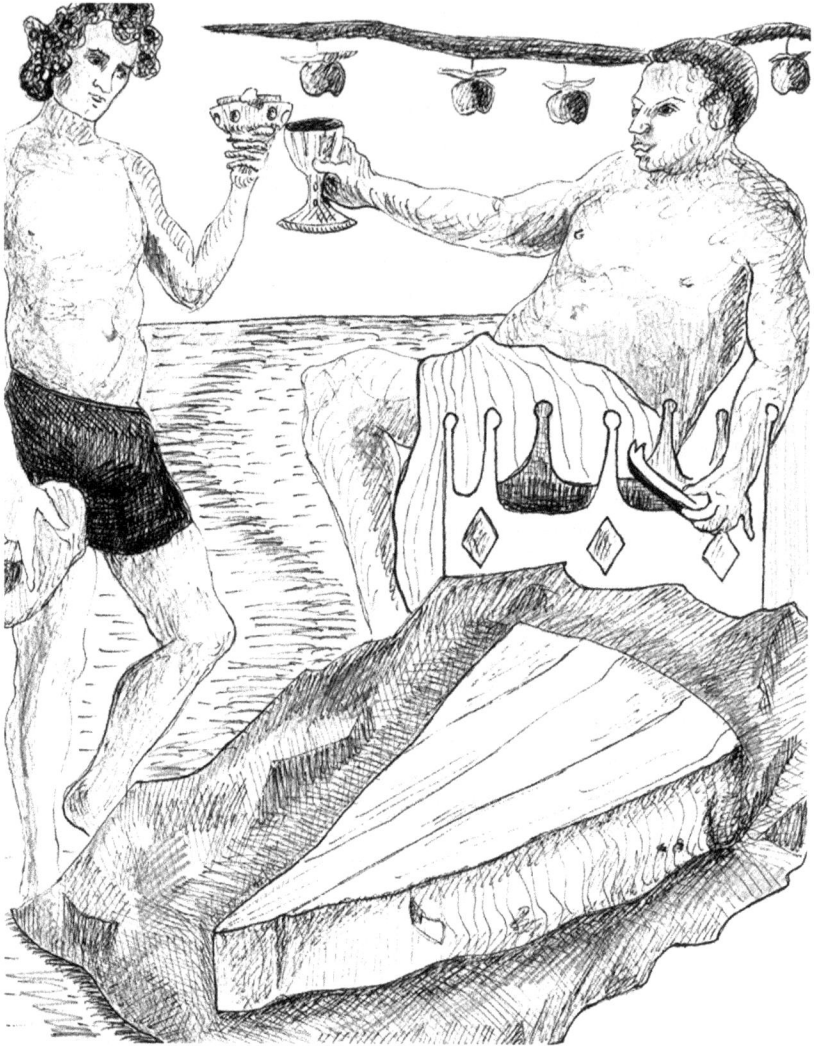

BRIE

Families and friends gather round

A more convivial cheese seldom found

But before you slice a piece take a look:

A large white round disk with streaks of red

Under its velvety rind a bewitching spread

With dough pale yellow like straw

On the palate a delicate delight

When ripened to perfection

The aromas makes one smile

The aftertaste lingers a while

Epicures know from long ago

The Brie was nominated king amongst its peers;

Therefore families take your time:

To hurry would be to commit a crime!

CAMEMBERT

Cows a supping in contented rhyme

Milkmaids with urns brimming to the rim

The curd ready; ladles poised

Moulds abound as the whey is drained

Turning, salting, part of the workday's toil

Nights and days spin their web of magical ways

Until at last a Camembert is spawned

Subtly salty, of creamy mushroom tang.

Marie Harel was her name

Taught by a priest

How to make a cheese of worldly fame

Boxed in spruce with a label to entice

Of fertile meadows with grasses green

Normandy thatched cottages proud to be seen.

Velvety coat of motley splendour

Exuberant of taste, runny on the tongue

To its praise we sing with hearty lung.

CHAOURCE

Vigorous champagne vineyards abound

Home to a cheese drum like in shape

Youthful and tender

With dough of snowy chalky splendour

Or ripened to gossamer melting delight

With a texture like butter

Causing the heart to flutter

Mature a little more

Runny to its zestful core

Champagne a neighbour full of pride

Make this cheese an excellent bride.

CÎTEAUX

By candle light in cellars profound
From a monastery buried in time
Cistercian monks casting shadows divine
Stirring the milk of their Montbeliard kine
They make a cheese of deserving renown
A dignified character of its own
Eaten by the locals in the countryside around
This precious treasure is seldom found
Its greyish yellow rind is washed in brine
Flaunting ambrosial flavours sublime
It is to the palate without doubt
A heavenly dish of praise devout

COMTÉ

When the wind whistles through mountain top

And the dark of winter carpets the valleys

Farmers share their Comté around a blazing hearth

A tradition from when knights fought for sacred causes.

This is a cheese from the milks of summer mountain pastures

Magnificent in size, five score litres of milk and more;

Matured for months in cellars humid and warm

It lies in state on spruce wood planks

Natural rind of golden yellow hue

A year gone by, the crust is satin brown

The dough is smooth, malleable with occasional tiny holes

A lofty taste, pithy with salt and fruity sensations

A royal feast that gives one palpitations

COULOMMIERS

C ow's raw milk

O rigin, Ile-de-France

U niform texture of the dough

L ight and sweet on the palate

O rangey streaks on the rind

M ushroom, truffles and garlic savours

M atured after eight weeks

I deal for a party

E njoyable throughout the year, particularly in
spring and autumn

R elated to the Brie

S tunning and succulent

Facts and figures give me the dithers
But a slither of this cheese
Satisfies all my needs

EPOISSES DE BOURGOGNE

Pulse and heart race with throb

Taste buds alive in full anticipation

No wonder Napoleon liked this creation

Four inches wide to one inch thick

In its youth, firm with tempting fascination

Pungent, spicy, saline of alchemy august

Taste sensuously velvety with majestic flavour

Dough the colour of creamy-blond

Washed in marc*, odours of perfumes bold

Matured a while a different smack

Tangy odours; creamy rustic

This cheese will make you lovesick.

Marc Marc brandy, its full name being eau-de-vie de Marc*
Distilled from Marc, the pulpy residue of any pressed fruit.

LAGUIOLE

A worthy tale.......the Laguiole has an interesting pedigree........it comes from
the fertile volcanic pastures of Auvergne...........local folklore dictates the
cheese was first made at the monastery in the plateau of Aubrac......the monks
taught cheese making to the local farmers known as burronniers...........this
word comes from buron, a mountain hut where the cheese is
made..........pause to image flower sprinkled mountain meadows filled with
fragrances of fennel and thyme...........today's cheese makers, during the
summer months, live in the Massif Central mountains with their herds of
Pie-Rouge-de-l'Est breed..........at one time the Aubac cow was
preferred.............the cheese is both magnificent in size and flavour.........the
shape is a large log that can weigh up to 50 kilograms............the
taste......complex, flowery, herby with a sharp tang...........cut the cheese
with a Laguiole knife......that is a story for another day.

LANGRES

Crinkly rind with a humid touch

Regularly washed in brine with heed

A cheese of particular shape

A soufflé with a dent on top

Fill with marc* or champagne

To enjoy a taste of different vein

Annatto dye added with flair

Gives the rind an orange grain

The dough: white verging on ecru

Aromas of vigorous strain

Spicy and of particular savour

A lemony zest teases the tongue

On the palate a creamy web is spun

They tell us the monks made it first

To day the farmers are well versed.

Marc marc bandy, its full name being eau-de-vie de marc
Distilled from marc, the pulpy residue of any pressed fruit.*

LIVAROT

Colonel* in name, not in shape

Five stripes of rush to hold it straight

Like an officer graded by rank

The Livarot well ripened has an elevated swank

Paraded with its Normandy cousins it compares

To a camembert, but more pungent

Provocative musky balminess with lingering smack

Apples and pears a flawless match

Once on the palate it relents to please

We salute you dear cheese

Please stand at ease.

*Colonel** The Livarot is known as 'the colonel' in France.*

MIMOLETTE

Cow's milk from the northern plains

Boule de Lille is another name

As a stripling, yellow to the core

But with age, carrot colour all the rage

A more solid cheese had you never

Bring a chisel to cut a chunk

Hard but brittle, tingling to the tongue

Fruity aroma, mellow aftertaste

Grate for cooking do not waste

Maturity renders the dough in its prime

Hack another chunk without wasting time.

MORBIER

The Morbier lies in wait;

The day's work is done

Comté made, but left is some

Protected by a layer of ash

The next day completes its fate;

The cheese is born full of grace

With rind dry and smooth

The dough of pale yellow taint

Yeasty savour, complex mordant flavour

Seductive taste of nuts and fruit

A pleasure we cannot dispute.

MUNSTER

Washed and rubbed in brine

The riper it becomes more pungent the scent

The taste buds it does torment

Made from cow's milk in which protein abounds

A rind of russet hue tells of sensations umpteen

Supple and creamy dough with bold embrace

Nutty, sweet, and complex that leaves a trace

Potatoes and cumin to give it relish

To make the feast a royal delight

A local wine from Alsace is just right.

NANTAIS

The French revolution in full assail

A priest in fear of his deathbed

To Nantes he fled

There he hid in secret abode

Working nights by candlelight

Magic in his hands with milk he made

A cheese that has lasted many decades;

Rind washed with sticky coat

Delectable dough, tantalizing taste

The celebrant left his mark

For all of us to remark.

NEUFCHÂTEL

Often shaped as a heart

A valentine gift for a sweetheart

The Neufchatel was born many centuries ago

In the Pays de Bray;

Napoleon III received as a gift

Made from cows' milk with piebald coats

Enriched from meadows on which they graze

This is a cheese from Normandy's glorious lands

The rind is soft and velvety to the touch

Its satiny oozing dough has a mushroom allure

A slice of bread is what one needs

For the gustative pleasure to sincerely succeed

PONT L'EVÊQUE

Created in the mists of time

By the monks in the Abbey d'Auge

With stately grace they named it Angelot;

This cheese is always square in form

Wrapped in paper, boxed in wood

Rind hard of crust, a protective case.

White when young; yellow with age

Washed and brushed perfect for a fete

The dough is pliant with sapid fragrance

Generous and savoury

Normandy is its domain

With a town of the same name.

REBLOCHON

History's mythology:....you be the judge.....the word Reblochon comes from reblocher meaning to pinch the cow's udder again....the second milking gives a thicker richer milk.....a farmer's delight...No! Some say the word comes from *reblessa* meaning to steal......here lies an old Savoyard story......at one time taxes were assessed by the amount of milk a Savoyard farmer could deliver to his customers.....when the tax inspector was present the cows were never completely milked.......once the undesirable character left, the cows were milked a second time.......the milk was found to be richer and made an excellent family cheese that could be enjoyed away from the prying eyes of tax inspectors......whichever story you prefer the Reblochon cheese was born........the result is a cheese well-proportioned (1 inch thick and 51/2 inches in diameter), presented in the form of squat round shape.......a thin orange color washed rind with a white velvety mould......a tender, ivory dough......sensations of freshness and sweetness stimulates the palate.......a delicate walnut aftertaste.......this is a cheese from mountain meadows of the 'Savoie'.

SAINT MARCELLIN

A yarn of woe five hundred years ago

The future King Louis XI a hunting he would go

A monstrous beast from the forest did abound

By a caper from his horse he fell to the ground

Two burly woodmen dallying in thickets coarse

Revived the Dauphin in due course

With a delectable treasure well found

A little cheese small and round

Rind of natural mould

Oozy dough with sensuous enchantment

Pithy and nutty;

The nobleman declared to my table it must go

A taste to relish, a fragrance to awe.

The Dauphin was right,

This is a cheese one cannot ignore.

SAINT NECTAIRE

Round with a rind of reddish grey hue

A heart of silky texture with suggestive lure

Pleasant tastes of hazelnuts and spices

Fruity to perfection, mellowed to entice

No wonder King Louis XIV enjoyed a slice.

Meadows abound with floral dreams

On which Salers' cows chew the cud

Matured in caves of volcanic rock

Darkness and humidity take their toll

Give this cheese a distinctive nose

One is transported into nature's heart

Succulent to its very central part

VACHERIN MONT D'OR

Silhouetted against an angry sky

Lies the massif of Mont d'Or.

Villages hidden in hilly passes

Surrounded by luxuriant pastures

Farmers tend their cattle of a special breed

Giving milks of unusual bouquet

Turned to cheese by some magic art

Presented in a box of aromatic bark

Its wrinkly reddish rind conceals a delicious creamy flow

Sublime and heady

Take a spoon and dig it in

Alchemy known to few, is it a sin?

No, continue to dig in.

*Rest with me on green foliage: we have ripe fruit,
soft chestnuts and plenty of fresh cheeses.*

Virgil, 42 BC

WAITING TO BE APPRECIATED

Monsieur Pinot Noir. *"I do so hate waiting. Most of my life I have been waiting for this moment."*

Mademoiselle Epoisse. *"I agree, I have been sitting here for two hours. I am starting to feel hot and bothered."*

Monsieur Pinot Noir. *"That sounds intriguing; I also feel my body temperature rising. This balmy atmosphere does wonders for the body fragrances. Can you detect the nature of my aromas?"*

Mademoiselle Epoisse fell silent while she concentrated on the question.

Madamoiselle Epoisse. *"You are very fruity. I think I can detect blackberries and black cherries. But I am not certain as your redolence is quite complex."*

Monsieur Pinot Noir. *"You have a fine nose. It`s a pity they did not decant me as my bouquet would be better appreciated. But tell me, my dear cheese, where do you come from?"*

Mademoiselle Epoisse. *"I come from the Côte-d'Or in France, not far from Dijon. My family`s origins go back to the 16th century."*

Monsieur Pinot Noir. *"How fascinating! I come from the same region."*

Mademoiselle Epoisse. *"Oh! That's astounding! There is a story in our family that Napoleon I was very partial to Epoisses (our family's name) and enjoyed us with a wine from Bourgogne. I think the wine was a Chambertin, but when I am tangy and provocative like this my memory tends to leave me."*

Monsieur Pinot Noir. *"I am a Chambertin. This should be a memorable evening. As both of us from the same region our savors will blend and compliment each other to perfection."*
With a frustrated tone, he added. *"Why hasn't the bread arrived?"*

Mademoiselle Epoisse. *"The bread is always late, something about being crisp and hot. Mind you I do love being wrapped in freshly baked bread."*

Monsieur Pinot Noir. *"My nose is beginning to tell me you are a zestful and pungent cheese. Maybe it is a good idea to wait for the bread; if not, you might be somewhat overpowering. A very tempting thought, but, for me, I think, a little frustrating."*

Mademoiselle Epoisse was just about to make a remark when Tom, the family cat, jumped up to the sideboard and cautiously dipped his front paw into the cheese. On the first taste the cat's long tail started lashing out in all directions knocking over the bottle of wine.

Above the sound of wine dripping down the side board and splashing on to the parquet floor a wounded Mademoiselle Epoisse faintly heard Mr. Pinot Noir cursing the freshly baked bread...

Bibliothèque Nationale, Paris

GOAT'S CHEESES

Have you ever seen a silly goat's smile?
Long rectangular faces with supercilious grins
Shaggy coats, with bristly beards
Hooves to boot with a vicious kick
Fleet of foot
But stubborn to the core
They wander free
Mountains, plains, all the same
Grasses, wild flowers they eat it all
Greedy is the word they know too well
But their milks are a transient treat
Their cheeses seasonal and vivacious
Snowy white dough under tender rind
Refreshing, stimulating tastes one always finds
Thank you dear goats, for being so kind.

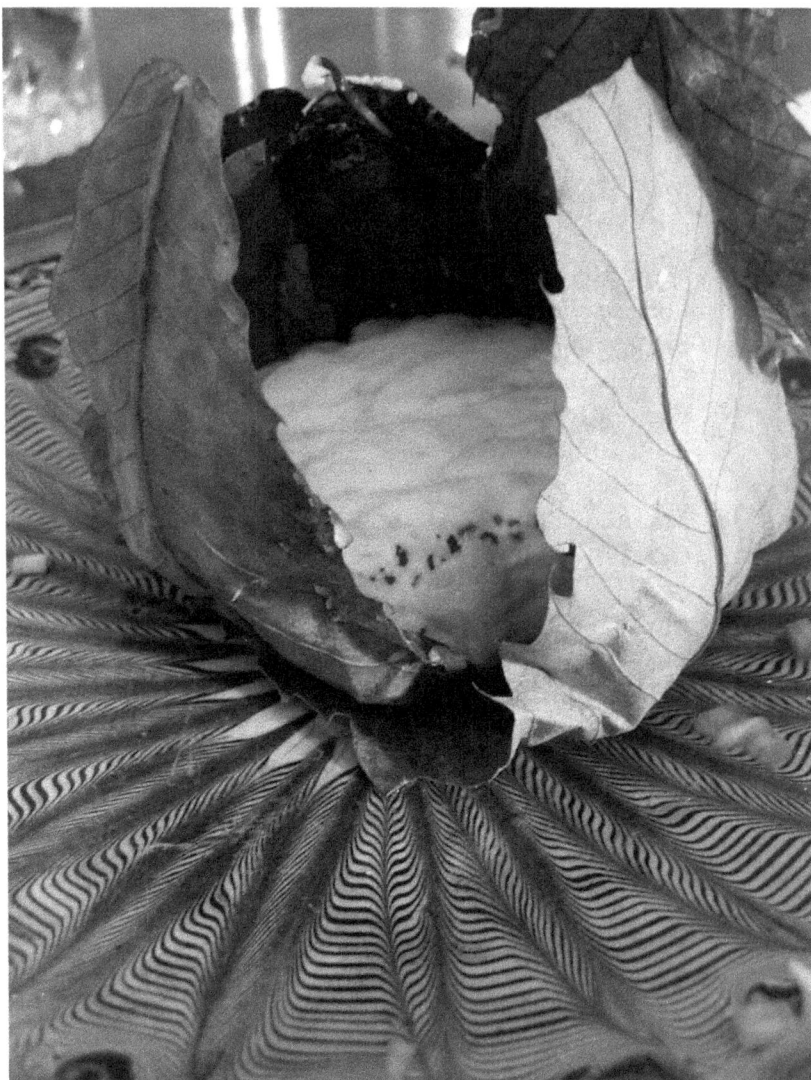

BANON À LA FEUILLE

Hiding in chestnut leaves

Tied with straw

Small and round

Its charm lies within

Succulently savoury

Enticingly endearing

Fruity to the core

Often bathed in marc*

Provocative to the tongue

A taste of rustic rapture

Provence is its kingdom

Parched lands of ancient dukedoms

Marc * marc bandy, its full name being eau-de-vie de marc distilled from marc the pulpy residue of any pressed fruit.

CABÉCOU DE ROCAMADOUR

Clothed in a thin rind with ductile dough

Minted like a coin, of bouquet well defined

Ripened two weeks a pleasurable treat

Unctuous, nutty, lactescent, harmonious and discrete

Matured six weeks a different take

Crumbly dough with fragrance strong

Rustic lactic savours lie hidden there

Perfectly wed with toasted bread,

A tingling tang with aroma intense

This is a cheese of pleasure immense.

In Languedoc dialect it means "little goat"

This, dear gourmets, is added as a footnote.

CROTTIN DE CHAVIGNOL

From ivory white to a golden patina

Lactic of goat`s ambrosia

Aging hardens the rind and changes the dough

The taste was soft, now brittle

Savors subtle, now robust

A cheese of character known to many ;

The young crottin is of unusual relish

Toast, salad, grilled on top

Partners seldom better found

Eaten young or after the passage of time

This cheese requires a good wine

POULIGNY-SAINT-PIERRE

Tall and pointed it stands

Like a pyramid from desert lands

On the eye a pure delight

Its colour of youth is all white

But with the passing of time

Its coat becomes more defined

Autumn complexion painted true

Mottled rind of brown and blue

A texture crinkled with age.

What secrets lie within?

The dough a flawless lily white

Sour and saline to the tongue

Taste buds alive and unstrung

SAINTE-MAURE DE TOURAINE

Rolled like a truncated log

With straw inserted for firm hold

A rind of natural mould

The dough white as crystals clear

The taste of goat's milk, piquant, bold

Salty, sourness as walnut balminess unfold

Gourmets gather round

This goat's cheese in Touraine is found

Majestic chateaus do there abound

Princely parks for elegant walks

Pastures basking in the summer sun and goats galore

Here one has a cheese of dignified allure

SELLES-SUR-CHER

S harp not soft and smooth

S avours aromas of walnuts

S alivate after the first taste

S ensations melt in the mouth

S apor of distinctive relish

S eductive: like all great goats cheeses

S cintillating: teases the taste buds

S prinkled with wood ash

S urprise snow-white dough

S cent of goats' milk

S easonal spring to autumn

S quat shaped in a round

S weet contrasted with salty sourness

S elles-sur-cher a savory splendour.

How can anybody be expected to govern a country with 325 cheeses?

General Charles de Gaulle

A STRANGE AND BEAUTIFUL
LOVE AFFAIR

There was no reason to suppose that they would fall in love. He was tall and ominous looking, she was squat and dumpy. The tall one had a healthy glow, as if he had spent all his life weathered by the mad winds of March and the kisses of the summer sun. She, by comparison, was pale with a beautiful motley skin that had a magical attraction which compelled one to want to touch her. She was definitely cuddly.

One enchanted evening they found themselves in a heated room placed next to one another. It must have been the warmth that had a peculiar effect on them. The cuddly one started feeling a strange movement in her body, she became soft, and slowly seductive perfumes exuded from her skin; then she had that delicious feeling of wanting to embrace her neighbour. The moment was even more delectable as she caught the fragrance of his wild and exotic fruits that were wafting over her skin. She looked across at her companion who stood tall and dignified at her side. Did she detect a slight movement in acknowledgement of her seductive efforts? Yes, a slight quiver, hardly discernable to the naked eye but in her heart she knew her efforts had been answered.

Later that night they came together in a union of innocent bliss.
The pleasure was overpowering.

The plates were clean and the last drop of wine poured...

Henry turned to his host and said.
   "That was a remarkable chaource with a superb Macon Blanc! An evening to remember" .

Bibliothèque Nationale, Paris

EWE'S CHEESES

Long sad faces
Eyes worthy of a cry
Tough short bodies
With stumpy legs that travel far
They roam the mighty plains of meagre fair
Seeking dainty dinners
Shepherds watch with careful eyes
Preying wolves prowling on the sly
Ewe in French is brebis
French for milk is lait
The 'lait de brebis' is a delectable delight
Flavourful, herby and enthralling
Making cheeses of uncommon taste
Prepared with care for our palates to embrace.

BRIN D'AMOUR

Born in the island of beauty

Rind coated in rosemary and thyme

Dough snow-white with brackish, herby tang

On the palate this cheese plays a merry tune

Heartstrings tighten; heads swoon

Perfume of herbs; aromatic on the tongue

A dainty shape round of form

True to its origins, Corsican in character

Its secret jealously hidden long ago

The name 'Amour' whispers love

To dreamily linger in the air above

A gift for Valentines, a handsome jest

The cheese deserves to be blessed.

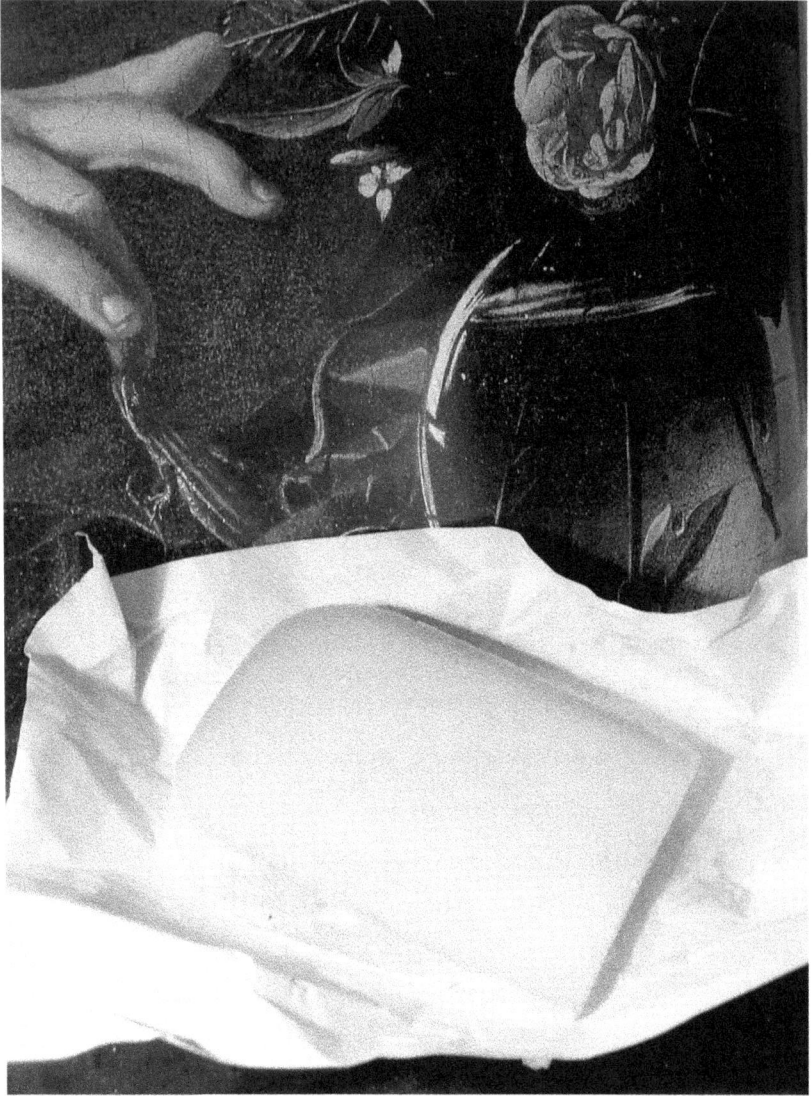

OSSAU-IRATY

High in the Pyrénées pastures

Murmuring winds in the mountains

The constant tinkling of animals' bells

Dogs corralling contented sleepy ewes

Shepherds herd their evening flocks

Fires are lit

The smell of cheese taints the air

Milk rich from the enchanted spell of the land

Flowers and herbs blessed by evening's dew

Born is the Ossau-Iraty of exalted grace

With a natural protective rind

Its golden dough yielding to the touch

On the palate the pleasure is delectably overmuch

ROQUEFORT

Dark and damp with drafty corridors

Hidden caves in limestone rock

Allows the cheese to ripen lost in time

This is the place where alchemy unfolds

Like blocks of rounded marble they stand

Proud and stately in silent pose

Their crumbly dough streaked with veins of blue

Palate and tongue tingle with delight

Lactescent, salty with complex tang

Force powerful images of wind swept lands

Herds of sheep in peaceful sleep

While shepherds watch over starry skies

Here in the Roquefort many mysteries lie.

TASTING TO ETERNITY

George sat at the head of the table; in fact, as the master of his manor, George always sat at the head of the table. This vantage point allowed him to survey the manners of his many children and look with pride upon his charming wife.

George took life seriously. He worked hard to keep the dinner table laden with a good fare. He was a cheese taster; his family, for generations, had always been cheese tasters. This noble profession consisted of finding, sampling and classifying as to gustative merit all the cheeses in his community that extended over ten square miles. The cheeses were mostly cheddar, but occasionally a few French cheeses found their way into his domain. To praise these foreign cheeses in a community where the country folk lived close to the land and were renowned for their excellent English cheddar would be, he had always considered, inappropriate. But his experience told him these were cheeses of exceptional savors and their diversity of taste quite remarkable.

With a look of consternation he glanced down the table at his eldest son, Charles. A youngster more interested in showing prowess on the sporting field than in his father's trade. Very disturbing, as in a few years, Charles was destined to take over the family business. As he groomed his handsome whiskers George's thoughts turned to his son's future. A little foreign travel would do him good. Why not Paris? He remembered the family had a distant cousin living somewhere near Rungis. George had never travelled out of his territory but he had heard many tales from various colleagues of how they could easily hide on the trains that had extensive rail network all over England and for that matter all over the continent. It should not be too difficult to organize.

Three days later Charles left for Paris armed with a good supply of cheddar and a letter to George's cousin setting out in detail the purpose of his eldest son's visit.

The journey was long, adventurous and at times quite dangerous and scary; for a mouse to travel so far is of noteworthy merit. Exhausted, Charles finally arrived at a large central station in the heart of Paris. There on the platform was Bernard an elderly, affable mouse with an infectious laugh and a well-rounded stomach supported by spindly legs.

As Charles stepped into Bernard's well-appointed cellar he was met with squeals of delight as the family gathered to welcome him. Bernard held up his paw for silence. Charles was formally introduced: more squeals of delight. Again Bernard called for silence. This time he read his cousin's letter for all to hear.

My dear cousin.

Although we have never met I am told you are just the right person to teach my son all about French cheeses. Occasionally we find French cheeses in our community and although personally I am convinced of their gustative merits, for diplomatic reasons, I consider them unsuitable for our consumption.

I presume one month will be ample time for my son to become familiar with all the cheeses available. You might find a month's stay unnecessary, if so, please send him home immediately.

It is well-known the fair city of Paris has many attractions that might distract Charles from the prime object of learning the art of appreciating cheese. I trust you will watch over him carefully.

Dear cousin, I send you some excellent English cheddar cheese in our appreciation of your hospitality.

Your cousin
Affectionately

George
Watershed village, Wiltshire.

Bernard put the letter down; the welcoming squeals had turned to the merry sound of laughter. "A month to taste all our cheeses!" Bernard said with a large grin on his face, "Charles, your dad has no idea of what is awaiting you. Tomorrow we will visit the cheese market at Rungis."
The early morning birds were already busy as Bernard, accompanied by one of his sons and Charles, left home. Minutes later the three mice stealthily tiptoed into the Rungis cheese market. The daily activity was in full swing with bargains and handshakes coming from all directions, trolleys laden with cheeses were being pushed across long corridors as buyers directed them to their waiting lorries. But what made Charles catch his breath was the mountains of cheeses that stretched as far the eye could see and, no doubt, to the end of the earth. He was overwhelmed, unable to speak.

Bernard took Charles's paw. "It's all right; I too, after all these years, am amazed by the sheer size of this market. They say it is the largest in the world."
Bernard continued in a whisper. "To make any sense of it, today I will start by giving you your first lesson on the various families of cheeses (fresh cheese, soft-ripened with velvety rind, washed rind, blue-veined, uncooked pressed, cooked pressed, goat's and processed cheeses). Then I will tell you about the various regions of France, after that the history of certain cheeses, followed by stories about the villages and personalities. It is only then we will start tasting."
Charles was at a loss to know how to reply, but he thought it was a lifetime's occupation and he would not be going home in the near future.

How right he was!

The poets have been mysteriously silent on the subject of cheeses.

GK Chesterton (1874-1936)

THE GOURMAND...

Recipes

Wine and Cheese

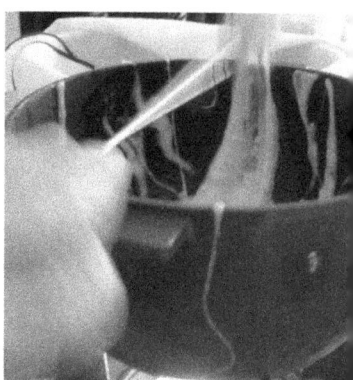

RECIPES

Cheese is probably the best of all foods
as wine is the best of all beverages.

Patience Gray 1957

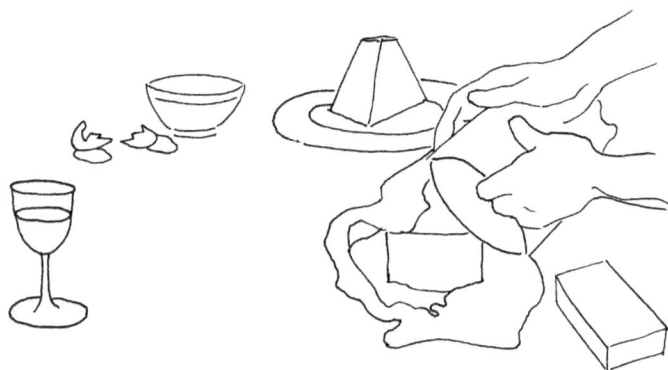

To the Kitchen I went
Time well spent
With sleeves rolled up high
Cheese dishes I made after many a try

Classical specialities came to mind
Imagination produced recipes unsigned
Tasting was a treat
I was careful not to overeat

The results hereby I show
Please, dear readers, enjoy with gusto
Don't forget the wine
When ready to dine

ALIGOT OF LAGUIOLE

serves 4

500g Laguiole
1kg potatoes
0.10l fresh cream
2 garlic cloves
50g butter

In a saucepan of cold water place the potatoes whole and unpeeled. Cook over a medium heat for 20 minutes or until they are entirely cooked. Drain then peel them.

Mash the potatoes in a heavy-bottomed saucepan, then add the cream and butter and incorporate thoroughly.

Cut the Laguiole into small pieces. Place the puree over a low heat and while stiring add the Laguiole and the crushed garlic.

Continue to stir the puree. The Aligot is ready when the Laguiole has completely melted through the puree and it has developed a smooth, elastic texture.

BEAUFORT SOUFFLÉ

makes 4

60g butter
50g flour
1/4l milk
200g Beaufort
50g Parmesan
4 eggs
1/2tbsp nutmeg
salt and ground black pepper

Preheat oven to 190°C.

Prepare four small soufflé dishes with butter and sprinkle evenly with Parmesan cheese.

In a saucepan melt the butter and add the flour and cook without browning for 2 minutes then add the milk, which has already been warmed in a separate saucepan. Stir and bring to the boil then remove from the heat. Allow to cool then add the egg yolks, nutmeg and the grated Beaufort. Blend thoroughly.

Whisk the egg whites to a frothy consistency. Add a spoonful of egg white to the cheese mixture and stir to loosen before folding the rest of the whites through.

Fill the prepared soufflé dishes and bake for 20-25 minutes until well risen and golden.

Serve immediately.

CABÉCOU AND MUSHROOM PATÉS

makes 4

500g fresh wild mushrooms,
several types if available or dried
porcini rehydrated and cultivated
mushooms
400g Cabécou
30g butter
1 egg
2 egg yolks
1/2 cup cream
25g chives
25g parsley
2 garlic gloves
olive oil
salt and ground black pepper

Preheat oven to 180°C.

Prepare 4 ramekin dishes of 7cm diameter with butter.

Slice the mushrooms then saute them in butter until they are cooked and all the moisture has evaporated. Add the finely diced garlic and chives and cook for another minute, then set aside.

In a bowl whisk the egg, the egg yolks, cream and the coarsely chopped parsley. Stir in the the roughly chopped Cabécou and the mushrooms. Salt and pepper to taste and then distribute the mixture between the ramekins.

Place in the oven and bake for approximately 30 minutes.

Remove from the ramekins and allow to cool slightly before serving.

FIGS STUFFED WITH CROTTIN DE CHAVIGNOL

serves 4

8 fresh figs
2 Crottin de Chavignol
400g fromage frais (fresh cheese)
200g mesclun salad
5tbsp olive oil
fresh thyme
1/4tbsp sherry vinegar
1/4tbsp red wine vinegar
salt and ground white pepper

Wash then pat dry the figs. Cut of the tops of each of the figs and put them aside. With a teaspoon remove the pulp of the figs being careful not to damage their skins.

In a bowl mix the pulp of the figs, the fromage frais and the 2 grated Crottin de Chavignol cheeses. Add the finely chopped thyme and one tablespoon of olive oil then season with salt and ground white pepper. Combine the mixture thoroughly.

Carefully fill each fig with the mixture then replace the top.

In a bowl make a vinaigrette with the remaining oil, the two vinegars and a pinch of salt and dress the mesclun salad, then serve together.

FONDUE FRANC-COMTOISE

serves 4

400g Comté
400g Vacherin Mont d'Or
500g crusty country bread
2 glasses white wine
1 large garlic clove
ground black pepper
nutmeg

Remove the rind from the Comté and cut into small pieces.

In a casserole dish add the white wine and the crushed garlic. Place over a low flame and cook slowly. When the liquid has heated entirely, add the Comté, portion at a time whilst stirring in a figure of eight. Season with ground black pepper and grated nutmeg according to taste.

Spoon in the Vacherin Mont d'Or when the Comté has completely melted, then reduce the flame. Never remove from the heat. Serve the fondue when the cheeses are thoroughly combined.

Cut the bread into small cubes.

In the center of the table prepare a heating surface, such as a raised hot plate placed over a low flame. This is neccesary to maintain the liquid consistency of the fondue.

To enjoy as a communal dish, each member of the table has a skewer to dip the cubes of bread into the fondue casserole.

GRATIN BRIARD

serves 4-6

1/4l milk
1/4l liquid cream
1 1/2kg potatoes
4 large garlic cloves
500g Brie
100g butter
salt and ground black pepper

Preheat oven to 200°C.

In a heavy-bottomed saucepan melt the butter and the finely diced garlic. Cook over a low heat, add 100g of Brie without its rind.

Peel and slice the potatoes. In a saucepan place the milk, cream and the potatoes, simmer for 10 minutes until the potatoes begin to soften. Season wih salt and ground black pepper.

Transfer the majority of the potatoes to a gratin dish or a shallow casserole dish. Ensure the potatoes are spread evenly in the dish then pour over the melted Brie and garlic. Place a final layer of potatoes, then cover with the remaining pieces of Brie without its rind.

Place in the oven and bake for 15 minutes until the Brie becomes golden, then serve.

LIVAROT AND MUSSEL OMELETTE

serves 2 to 4

30g Livarot
200g mussels
50g seaweed (optional)
6 eggs
20g butter
3 bay leaves
2 shallots
2 glasses of white wine
olive oil
salt and ground black pepper

Clean and debeard the mussels.

In a saucepan add the olive oil and the sliced shallots. Cook for 5 minutes until the shallots have softened. Add the wine, bay leaves and mussels and a spinkle of black pepper. Cover the saucepan and leave to simmer for 5 minutes over a low heat, shaking occasionally.

Drain the mussels through a colinder. Then remove them from their shell.

Remove the rind of the Livarot and cut into small cubes.

In a bowl whisk the eggs and season with salt and ground black pepper. Add the mussels, cubes of Livarot and the finely shredded seaweed.

In a flat saucepan melt the butter. Pour the mixture into the pan stirring the mixture out evenly.

Cook until the base is golden brown and the top is just set, then serve.

FRESH PASTA WITH PEAS AND POULIGNY-SAINT-PIERRE

serves 4

400g flour
4 eggs
300g shelled peas
300g Pouligny-Saint-Pierre
1 large leek
olive oil
2 glasses dry white wine
2 cups vegetable stock
salt and ground black pepper

To prepare the pasta: combine the flour and eggs to make a dough adding extra flour or water if needed to obtain a kneedable dough. Kneed for several minutes on a floured board. Roll out the dough until it is thin enough and then cut into lengths of approximately 1-2mm widths. The preparation of the pasta can also be done with a pasta machine.

To prepare the sauce: clean then thinly slice the leek. Cook over a medium to low heat in a saucepan with olive oil. Do not brown. Add the peas and the vegetable stock and simmer for 5 minutes. Pass through a sieve and retain the cooking liquid.

Puree three quarters of the peas and leeks. In a saucepan return the stock to the heat, add the wine and reduce to half.

Add the puree to the stock to make a sauce and bring to a simmer. Remove from heat, then add the remaining peas and leeks and season with salt and pepper.

Meanwhile, in a large saucepan bring plenty of salted water to the boil, add the pasta and cook for 5 minutes or until the pasta is 'al dente'. Strain the pasta.

Distribute the pasta and spoon the sauce over it. Remove the rind of the Pouligny-Saint-Pierre and crumble over each serving.

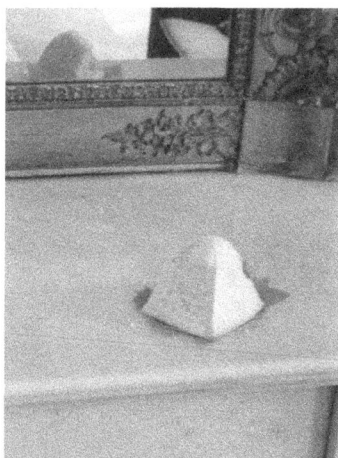

115

PRUNES WITH BEAUFORT

makes 16

16 prunes
100g Beaufort
16 slices bacon
1tsp black tea
16 cocktail sticks

Wash the prunes. Place the tea and the prunes in a saucepan and cover with water. Allow to simmer for 5 minutes, then remove from the heat. Leave to marinate over night. Strain the prunes from the tea and remove their stones.

Preheat the grill or oven to 250°C.

Cut the Beaufort into pieces a similar size to fit into the cavity of the prune. In each prune place a piece of Beaufort, then wrap with a slice of bacon and pin the bacon with a cocktail stick.

Place the prunes under the grill or in the oven for 3-5 minutes until the cheese melts and the bacon begins to crisp.

Allow to cool for 5 minutes, then serve.

QUICHE WITH MUNSTER

serves 6

250g flour
150g butter
7 egg
2 cups water
1 cup fresh cream
250g Munster
2 leeks
150g diced bacon
nutmeg
salt and ground black pepper

Preheat oven to 200°C.

To prepare the pastry: dig a well in the center of the flour, add a pinch of salt, 1 egg and 120g of softened butter. Add a cup of water then kneed to form a dough, add more water if needed to obtain a kneedable consistancy. Place the dough in the refrigerator for at least 10 minutes before use.

Roll out the pastry dough to approximately 30cm diameter and then set it into a buttered tart dish of a slightly smaller diameter. Prick the base of the pastry dough with a fork. To prevent from rising, cover with aluminium foil or baking paper and place on top a weight such as dried beans or rice. Cook in the oven for 5 minutes. Remove the weight and covering and cook for a further 5 minutes.

To prepare the filling: Clean then thinly slice the leeks. In a saucepan add 30g of butter and cook the leeks over a low heat for 2-5 minutes. Do not brown. Add a glass of water and continue to cook for another 5 minutes until the leeks have softened completely. Then remove from the saucepan and put aside. In another saucepan cook the diced bacon until it becomes crisp. Remove excess fat then set aside.

In a bowl whisk together the remaining 6 eggs and fresh cream. Season with grated nutmeg, salt and ground black pepper. Then add the bacon and leeks. Remove the rind of the Munster and cut into small slices. Evenly distribute the Munster over the pastry base, then cover with the mixture.
Bake for 45 minutes, then serve.

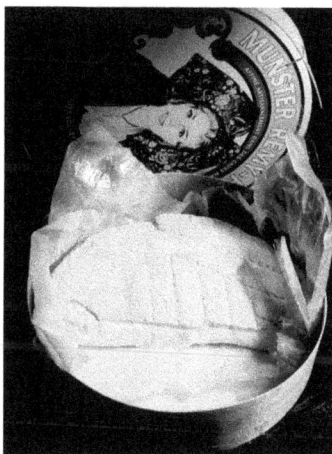

SHALLOT AND ROQUEFORT TARTLETS

makes 15-20

150g butter
225g flour
100g Roquefort
12 shallots
30g brown sugar
olive oil
salt and ground black pepper

To prepare the flaky pastry: place the butter in the freezer for 30 minutes. When the butter is ready, sieve the flour into a bowl and add a pinch of salt. Coarsely grate the butter. Then, using a knife, mix together the flour and butter. Add approximately one half of a cup of cold water, continue mixing to form a soft dough. Roll out the dough to form a disc and refrigerate for one hour.

To prepare the filling: peel the shallots and cut into quarters length ways. Heat olive oil in a pan, then add the shallots, a pinch of salt, pepper and brown sugar. Cook slowly until they have browned and caramelised.

Preheat oven to 180°C.

Roll the pastry to 4mm thickness and cut out the circles the size of the tartlet pans.

On each of the tartlet bases place a weight such as beans or rice to prevent from rising, then bake in the oven for approximately 10 minutes until golden brown. Remove the weight and the tartlets from the tartlet pans. Allow to cool slightly before filling.

Puree three quarters of the caramelised shallots. Place one tablespoon of the pureed shallots into each shell. Then crumble a small portion of the Roquefort over the puree. To finish place a small segment of the remaining shallots on each tartlet, then serve.

SELLES-SUR-CHER SOUP
WITH HAZELNUTS

serves 4

250g Selles-sur-cher
160g leg of lamb
1 egg yolk
0.60l milk
15g hazelnuts
olive oil
salt and ground black pepper

Preheat four shallow soup bowls in an oven of 150°C.

Crush the hazelnuts into little pieces. Cut the lamb into small cubes of approximately 5mm to 1cm. In a bowl, mix the cubed lamb, the egg yolk and three quarters of the crushed hazelnuts. Season with salt and pepper. With your hands form approximately 20 balls.

In a large saucepan heat some olive oil. Cook the lamb balls for approximately 10 minutes until brown on all surfaces.

Place each of the lamb balls on some absorbent paper to remove excess oil and fat.

Remove the rind of the Selles-sur-cher and cut into small pieces. Place the Selles-sur-cher and the milk in a saucepan and cook over a low heat, stir occasionally. Season with salt and ground black pepper. When the cheese has completely melted through it is ready to serve.

Equally distribute the lamb balls into each of the shallow bowls. Pour the soup over the lamb balls then sprinkle with the remaining crushed hazelnuts, serve immediately.

WINE & CHEESE

The forthright and at the same time subtle flavour of cheese stimulates the taste buds and readies them for wine. Wine in turn permits cheese to attain unimaginable heights of flavour. These two fruits of the earth were made for one another.

Pierre Androuet

If I had but one wish
On summer's day I would lie
Contented to languish
And contemplate the sky
When hunger beacons
In hand I take
A bottle of wine with a cheese on a plate
At first sip I know
The pleasure it bestows
Now the cheese I taste
Slowly without haste
Then together the union is formed
Savours and flavours on my palate spawn
When secrets unfold therewith, nature's gift to man
The odyssey with cheese and wine has just began.

Roussette de Savoie

Chablis

Chignin-Bergeron

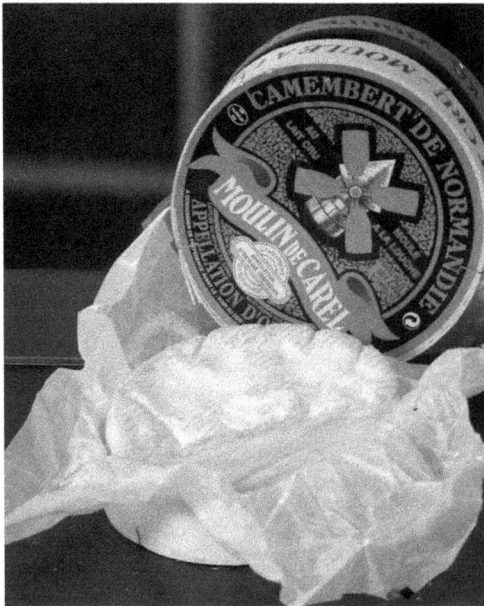

Rasteau

Saint-Emilion

Cidre

Beaujolais

Pomerol

Santenay

Sancerre

Riesling

Coteaux-d'Aix

Pommard

Pouilly-Fuissé

Chambertin

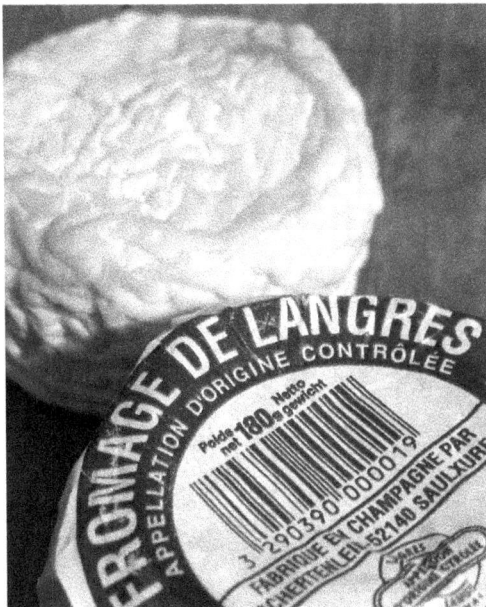

Champagne

Côtes du Rhône

Nuits-Saint-Georges

Marcillac

Buzet

Côtes du Rhône

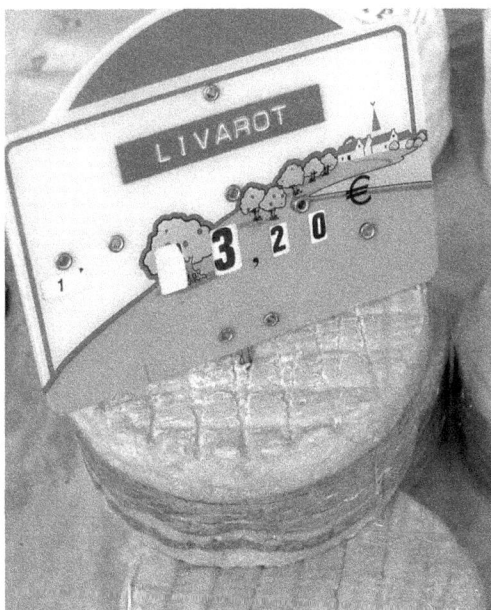

Pommard

Tokay

Calvados

Côtes-du-Jura

Vin blanc de Savoie

Saint-Julien

Madiran

Champagne

Jurançon

Juliénas

Gewurztraminer

Saint-Chinian

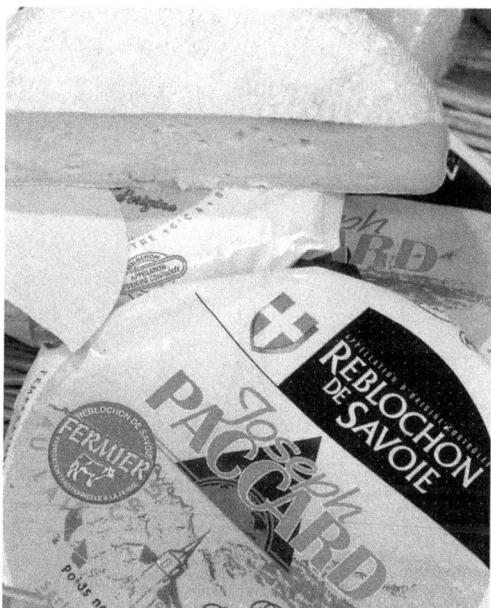

Crépy

Pommard

Vin blanc de Savoie

Sauternes

Châteauneuf-du-Pape

Monbazillac

Chiroubles

Saint-Emilion

Condrieu

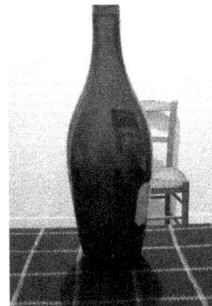

Bourgogne Aligoté

Chinon rouge

Gamay de Touraine

Bourgueil

Touraine blanc

Chinon

THE EPICURE...

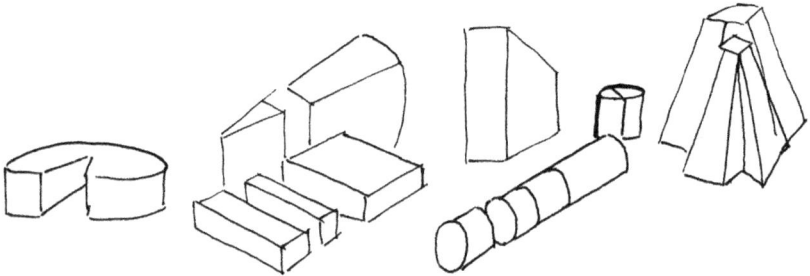

Essential Facts

COW'S CHEESES	PERIOD OF EXCELLENCE	WEIGHT	MATURATION
Beaufort	SPRING SUMMER AUTUMN WINTER	40kg	12–18 months
Brie	SUMMER AUTUMN	1.5 – 2kg	8–10 weeks
Camembert	SUMMER	250g	3–4 weeks
Chaource	SUMMER	250 – 450g	6–10 weeks
Cîteaux	SUMMER	700g	4–6 weeks
Comté	SPRING SUMMER AUTUMN WINTER	30 – 40kg	12–18 months
Coulommiers	SUMMER AUTUMN	400 – 750g	4 weeks
Epoisses	SUMMER AUTUMN	270 – 1100g	at least 4 weeks
Laguiole	SPRING SUMMER AUTUMN WINTER	30 – 50kg	6–32 months
Langres	SUMMER	180 – 700g	15–21 days
Livarot	SUMMER AUTUMN	450g	3 weeks
Mimolette	SPRING SUMMER AUTUMN WINTER	2 – 4kg	6 weeks–2 years
Morbier	AUTUMN	5 – 9kg	2–3 months
Munster	SUMMER AUTUMN	625g	8–9 weeks
Nantais	SUMMER	170 – 200g	1 month
Neufchâtel	SUMMER	100 – 200g	3 weeks
Pont l'Evêque	SUMMER	250 – 390g	5–6 weeks
Reblochon	SUMMER	240 – 500g	5–6 weeks

		WEIGHT	MATURATION
Saint Marcellin	SUMMER	30g	3 weeks
Saint Nectaire	SUMMER	1750g	8–10 weeks
Vacherin Mont d'Or	SUMMER	500 – 1000g	4–5 weeks

GOAT'S CHEESES	PERIOD OF EXCELLENCE	WEIGHT	MATURATION
Banon à la feuille	SUMMER AUTUMN	90 – 120g	2 weeks–1 month
Cabécou de Rocamadour	SPRING SUMMER	30g	10–15 days
Crottin de Chavignol	SPRING SUMMER AUTUMN	90g	2–3 weeks
Pouligny-Saint-Pierre	SPRING SUMMER	250g	3–4 weeks
Sainte-Maure de Touraine	SPRING SUMMER	250g	3–4 weeks
Selles-sur-Cher	SPRING SUMMER	125 – 180g	3 weeks

EWE'S CHEESES	PERIOD OF EXCELLENCE	WEIGHT	MATURATION
Brin d'Amour	SPRING SUMMER	625 – 875g	at least a month
Ossau-Iraty	SPRING SUMMER AUTUMN	2 – 7kg	4–6 months
Roquefort	 SPRING SUMMER AUTUMN WINTER	2.5 –2.9kg	4–6 months

COW'S CHEESES
Les fromages de vache

The majority of French cheeses are made from cows' milk and are available the year round. The quantity of milk needed for a cheese varies considerably: a Camembert 2.3 litres of milk; a Comté 530 litres, the daily production of 30 cows.

The art of cheese making lies in the treatment of the milks: cooked or uncooked, pressed or unpressed, the way in which the curds are cut, method of salting, maturing, will all effect the way the cheese tastes. Examples:

Livarot, uncooked, unpressed with washed rind; Beaufort, cooked and pressed.

The transformation of the milk continues with the alchemy of ripening (affinage). Examples:

Pont-l'Evêque, two to six weeks; Mimolette: six months to two years.

The diversity and complexity of traditional French cheeses attest to the imagination and skill of the producers.

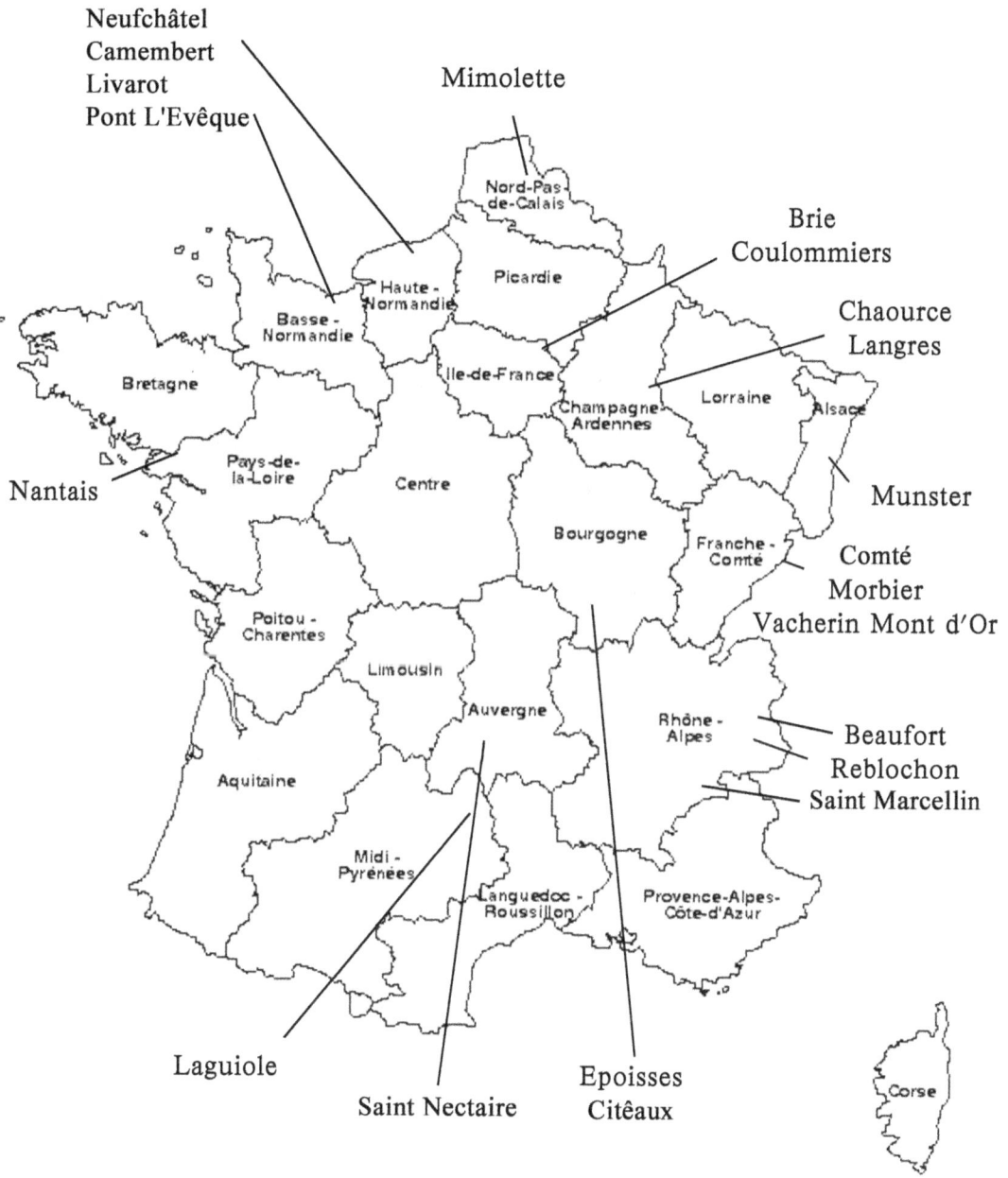

Neufchâtel
Camembert
Livarot
Pont L'Evêque

Mimolette

Brie
Coulommiers

Chaource
Langres

Nord-Pas-
de-Calais

Picardie

Haute-
Normandie

Basse-
Normandie

Ile-de-France

Lorraine

Alsace

Bretagne

Champagne-
Ardennes

Munster

Nantais

Pays-de-
la-Loire

Centre

Bourgogne

Franche-
Comté

Comté
Morbier
Vacherin Mont d'Or

Poitou-
Charentes

Limousin

Auvergne

Rhône-
Alpes

Beaufort
Reblochon
Saint Marcellin

Aquitaine

Midi-
Pyrénées

Languedoc-
Roussillon

Provence-Alpes-
Côte-d'Azur

Corse

Laguiole

Saint Nectaire

Epoisses
Citêaux

143

GOAT'S CHEESES
Les fromages de chèvre

Goats give birth to their young between January and March every year. Therefore the first milks after birth come from the lush spring grasses of April and May and continue through the summer months from grazing on sun baked pastures. This is the period when these cheeses are at their best. The maturing (affinage) period of goats' cheeses produces a variety of different flavours for all tastes from young fresh creamy to more mature dough that is brittle and flaky with a distinctive pronounced savour.

The various shapes of goat cheese attests to the imagination of the producers: bells, pyramids, hexagons, corks, truncated logs, thimbles, buttons, bricks. These cheeses are often sprinkled with herbs or ash and sometimes dusted with spices.

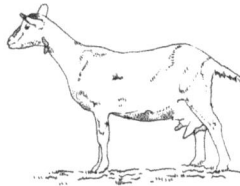

Nord-Pas-de-Calais

Picardie

Haute-Normandie

Basse-Normandie

Bretagne

Ile-de-France

Lorraine

Alsace

Champagne-Ardennes

Pays-de-la-Loire

Centre

Bourgogne

Franche-Comté

Selles-sur Cher
Pouligny-Saint-Pierre
Sainte-Maure de Touraine
Crottin de Chavignol

Poitou-Charentes

Limousin

Auvergne

Rhône-Alpes

Aquitaine

Midi-Pyrénées

Languedoc-Roussillon

Banon

Provence-Alpes-Côte-d'Azur

Cabécou
de Rocamadour

Corse

EWE'S CHEESES
Les fromages de brebis

One cannot talk about the savours of brebis cheeses without
mentioning the yearly transhumance movement of flocks. It
begins on the 24th June, Saint-Jean's day, when the ewes are
driven to the high mountain pastures and ends with the first
snows of October. In the past the flocks were herded by
shepherds and their dogs; today most herds are transported by
large double tiered lorries. These summer cheeses reflect the
succulent savours of the floral and herby high summer pastures.

Nord-Pas-de-Calais

Picardie

Haute-Normandie

Basse-Normandie

Bretagne

Ile-de-France

Champagne-Ardennes

Lorraine

Alsace

Pays-de-la-Loire

Centre

Bourgogne

Franche-Comté

Poitou-Charentes

Limousin

Auvergne

Rhône-Alpes

Aquitaine

Midi-Pyrénées

Languedoc-Roussillon

Provence-Alpes-Côte-d'Azur

Corse

Ossau-Iraty

Roquefort

Brin d'Amour

FRENCH CHEESE FAMILIES

Fresh cheeses
Fromages Frais et Fromages Blancs

These cheeses are uncooked and unripened. To be enjoyed soon after production.

Soft riped cheeses
Fromages à croûte fleurie

Semi-soft dough, their rinds are velvety with natural mould.

Washed-rind cheeses
Fromages à croûte lavée

The rind of these cheeses is regularly rubbed and washed with a solution of brine or another suitable liquid such as grape brandy.

Blue-veined cheeses
Fromages à pâte persillée

These are uncooked, unpressed cheeses that during the maturing period, are injected with penicillium roqueforti which develops the blue moulding.

Uncooked, pressed cheeses
Fromages à pâte pressée non cuite

These cheeses have been pressed to drain away the whey.

Cooked and pressed cheeses
Fromages à pâte pressée cuite

These cheeses are made from curd that has been heated before pressing.

Goat's cheeses
Fromages de Chèvre

Natural-rind cheeses with no washing or microflora.

examples; *Brocciu Corse A.O.C, Boursin à l'ail,*
Brousse du Rove...

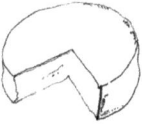

examples; *Brie, Camembert, Chaource,*
Coulommiers, Neufchatel, Saint Marcellin...

examples; *Epoisses, Langres, Livarot, Maroilles,*
Mont d'Or, Munster, Pont l'Evêque...

examples; *Roquefort, Bleu d'Auvergne, Bleu de*
Causses, Bleu de Gex, Fourme d'Ambert...

examples; *Cantal, Ossau-Iraty, Salers, Morbier,*
Tomme de Savoie...

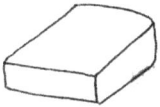

examples; *Comté, Beaufort, Emmental...*

examples; *Chabichou, Crottin de Chavignol,*
Pouligny-Saint-Pierre, Selles-sur-Cher...

CHEESE KNIVES

Grand couteau

Couteau à fourche

Petit Couteau

Couteau à chèvre

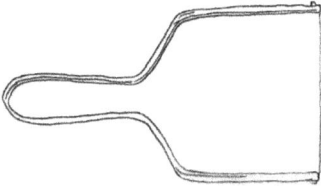

Lyre

Poiçon à Parmesan

Hachette à Hollande

Couteau Copeaux

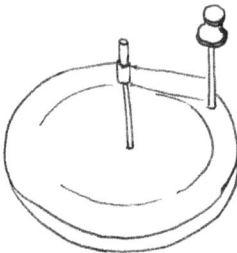

Girolle

Rabot à Sbrinz

CUTTING THE CHEESE

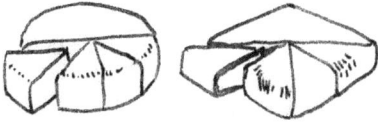

Camembert, Pont l'Evêque...

Beaufort, Emmental...

Roquefort...

Ossau-Iraty, Saint Nectaire...

Pouligny-Saint-Pierre, Chabichou...

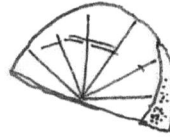

Mimolette...

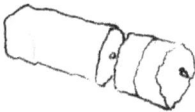

Sainte-Maure de Touraine

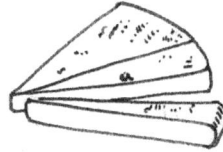

Brie, Coulommiers...

Banon à la feuille

Vacherin Mont d'Or

APPELLATION D'ORIGINE CONTRÔLÉE (AOC)

AOC guarantees that the product of quality has been produced within a specific region abiding by specific and established methods of production. AOC cheeses will indicate the fact on the labelling. Today there exists 42 AOC cheeses; 28 cow cheeses, 11 goat cheeses and 3 ewe cheeses.

-Jan 2007-

Cow's Cheeses

Abondance
Beaufort
Bleu d'Auvergne
Bleu de Gex
Bleu des Causses
Bleu du Vercors-Sassenage
Brie de Meaux
Brie de Melun
Camembert de Normandie
Cantal
Chaource
Comté
Epoisses
Fourme d'Ambert

Fourme de Montbrison
Laguiole
Langres
Livarot
Maroilles
Vacherin Mont d'Or
Morbier
Munster
Neufchâtel
Pont l'Evêque
Reblochon
Saint Nectaire
Salers
Tome des Bauges

Goat's Cheeses

Banon
Cabécou de Rocamadour
Chabichou du Poitou
Chevrotin
Crottin de Chavignol
Pelardon

Picodon
Pouligny Saint-Pierre
Sainte-Maure de Touraine
Selles-sur-Cher
Valencay

Ewe's Cheeses

Brocciu
Ossau-Iraty

Roquefort

TASTING TO ETERNITY...

PLEASURE ON THE PLATE, PLEASURE ON THE PALATE

Yes, I have seen mountain meadows and the lush grasses on the plains

Yes, I have felt the rains, been warmed by the sun, and tumbled in the snows

Yes, I have stood in the mad winds of March and been enveloped in autumn's mists

Yes, I have learnt these weather patterns paint their magic on nature's lands

Yes, I have seen nonchalant cows, ewes and sheep grazing

Yes, I know cheese is made out of their milk

Yes, I realize a well-matured cheese with its smell, touch and taste is pure alchemy

Yes, my eyes delight at the mellow colors, streaks of blue, and particular shapes

Yes, my fidgety fingers sense a soft texture or a hard protective crust

Yes, when the cheese is cut I marvel at the creamy dough, snow white or of golden hue

Yes, the odour fills my nostrils with country scents of the rich earth turned to face the sun

Yes, I know the first taste is creamy, subtly salty with a touch of earthly herbs

Yes, it slithers on my palate waking taste buds long forgotten

Yes, I feel a deep sensuous sensation in the recesses of my tongue

Yes, I experience epicurean delights seldom known to mortals

Yes, I feel overwhelmed by some divinely complex succulent taste

Yes, the savour lingers, teasing, tantalizing; impelling the flavour to indescribable heights

Yes, my pulse quickens; words cannot describe my state

Yes, I have lost all sense of time; minutes pass the pleasure lingers on

Yes, uncontrollably my body cries out for more

Yes, yes and again yes.

Acknowledgements

The author would like to extend his warm thanks to:

Tamar: Photographs and recipes

Jean David: Drawings

Fromages.com: Inspiration

French cheese makers: Their products

Our gentle creatures: Their milks

Imprimé sur papier recyclé

N° ISBN 978-2-9530136-0-3

IMP. MARIE - HONFLEUR • 02 31 89 20 34

www.ingramcontent.com/pod-product-compliance
Lightning Source LLC
Chambersburg PA
CBHW050352100426

42739CB00015BB/3366